May I Quote You, General Longstreet?

MAY I QUOTE YOU, GENERAL LONGSTREET?

Observations and Utterances of the South's Great Generals

Randall Bedwell

CUMBERLAND HOUSE

PUBLISHING INC.

Published by Cumberland House Publishing, Inc., 431 Harding Industrial Drive, Nashville, Tennessee 37211.

Some quotations have been edited for clarity and brevity.

Typography: The Booksetters Company
Cover design: Patterson Graham Design Group, Memphis, Tennessee
Text design: The BookSetters Company

Library of Congress Cataloging-in-Publication Data
May I quote you, General Longstreet? : observations and utterances of the
   South's greatest generals / [compiled by]Randall Bedwell.
      p. cm. —(May I quote you, General? series)
   ISBN 1-888952-37-7 (pbk.)
      1. Longstreet, James, 1921-1904—Quotations. 2. United States—
History—Civil War, 1961-1965—Quotations, maxims, etc. 3. Quotations
American. I. Bedwell, Randall J. I Series.
E467.1L55M39 1997
973.7'3'092—dc   96-51928
                                                                CIP

Table of Contents

Introduction

General James Longstreet has been called one of the great soldiers of American history. A man renowned for his cool demeanor under fire and winning military tactics, Longstreet quickly rose through the Confederate ranks to become Robert E. Lee's second in command. He was a warrior who appreciated the cost of war and was loath to sacrifice his men for victory if that victory held no strategic advantage. But when engaged, his resolve was unshakable, and he led his troops in the Army of Northern Virginia to glory.

Admired and trusted by his subordinates and superiors in gray and respected by his contemporaries in blue, Longstreet's defaming during

Introduction

Reconstruction overshadowed his reputation and deeply troubled the general. Detractors claimed that Longstreet's disastrous attack at Gettysburg was contrary to Lee's orders and led to a Rebel defeat that ultimately doomed the Confederate cause. Moreover, Longstreet was labeled a traitor for accepting an office during Grant's presidency. Neither Lee's accounts nor official records supported the accusations, yet they became accepted as part of popular wisdom.

Longstreet battled the allegations of his accusers until he died, staunchly maintaining that his actions were honorable and borne out of loyalty to his commander and the South. The man General Lee called "the staff of my right hand" thus became dogged by controversy, forced to fight his enemies years after his comrades had laid down their arms.

Randall Bedwell
Cordova, Tennessee
November 1996

Longstreet, not Jackson, was the finest corps commander in the Army of Northern Virginia; in fact, he was arguably the best corps commander in the conflict on either side.

—*Jeffrey Wert, James Longstreet's biographer*

CHAPTER ONE

Divided Loyalties

When the clouds of war gathered darkly on the horizon, Major James Longstreet, like General Robert E. Lee and numerous other glorious leaders of the South, was an officer in the army of the United States. Had his allegiance remained with the Union, high command awaited him, promising a splendid future of fame, honor, and rich rewards. Heeding the call of the South meant a far less certain future; yet Longstreet did not hesitate to offer his sword for his homeland. Although opposed to the idea of secession, his devotion and unwavering

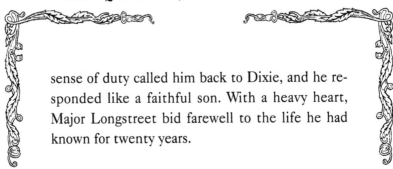

sense of duty called him back to Dixie, and he responded like a faithful son. With a heavy heart, Major Longstreet bid farewell to the life he had known for twenty years.

★ ★ ★

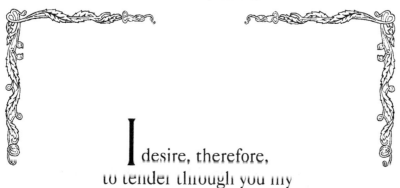

I desire, therefore, to tender through you my services to her, should she need a soldier who has seen hard service. I am the senior officer of the Army, from Alabama, and should be the first to offer her such assistance in my profession as I may be able to render.

—*General Longstreet in a letter to Alabama Governor Andrew B. Moore, February 1861*

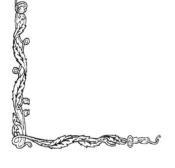

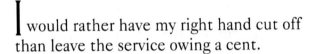

I would rather have my right hand cut off than leave the service owing a cent.

—*General Longstreet on his delay to join the Confederacy until his obligations to the Federal army were complete*

A t least three years, and if it holds for five you may begin to look for a dictator.

—*General Longstreet, when asked about the length of the impending war*

I came to the South because I feared that it might not be able to do well without me. I had more experience in battle, or thought that I had, than any other man North or South and was apprehensive that our people could not get along without me. I had no ambition to gratify nor have I any now more than to discharge my duties.

—General Longstreet in a letter to General D. H. Hill, March 1864

James Longstreet

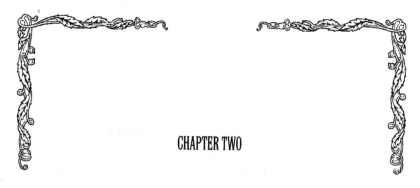

CHAPTER TWO

The Undismayed Warrior

Longstreet realized even more success in the army of the Confederacy than he had seen in service to the Union. He rapidly rose from the rank of major to that of lieutenant general and second in command to General Lee. Under his command, the Army of Northern Virginia gained its reputation as the greatest fighting army the world had ever seen. At Bull Run, the Seven Days' battles, Second Manassas, Antietam, Fredericksburg, Chickamauga,

the Wilderness, and in nearly every principal battle and victory of the South, there was Longstreet
leading his men to glory.

James Longstreet was a soldier who faithfully
served and a leader who bravely led, and he
quickly earned a reputation as one of the hardest
fighters in the Army of Northern Virginia. Always
calm, even in the midst of battle, it would be said
that he was like a rock in his steadiness. His clear
head and brave heart inspired his men to unparal-
leled deeds of valor.

By his presence at the
right place at the right moment
among his men, by the exhibition of
characteristic coolness, and by his words
of encouragement to the men of his command, he infused a confidence and spirit
that contributed largely to the success
of our arms on that day.

—General Pierre Gustave Beauregard on
General Longstreet after Blackburn's Ford

[Longstreet] amid a perfect shower of balls, rode amongst them with his cigar in his mouth, rallying them, encouraging, and inspiring confidence among them.

—*Major Thomas Goree on General Longstreet*
at Bull Run

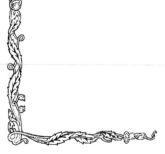

Retreat! Hell, the Federal Army has broken to pieces!

—*General Longstreet on receiving orders*
to withdraw from Centerville

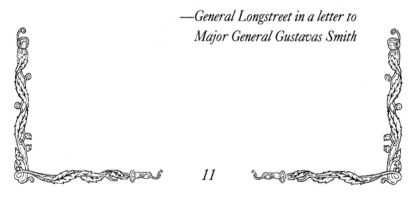

If he is ever excited, he has a way of concealing it, and always appears as if he has the utmost confidence in his own ability to command and in that of troops to execute.

—Major Thomas Goree describing Longstreet in a letter to his mother, December 1861

I don't fear McClellan or any one in Yankeedom.

—General Longstreet in a letter to Major General Gustavas Smith

Well, McCall is safe in Richmond; but if his division had not offered the stubborn resistance it did on this road, we would have captured your whole army. Never mind. We will do it yet.

—*General Longstreet to a Federal prisoner,*
Seven Days' Campaign

My affection for him is unfailing. Such efficiency on the field as I may have displayed came from association with him and the example of that undismayed warrior. He was like a rock in steadiness when sometimes in battle the world seemed flying to pieces.

—*Brigadier General G. Moxley Sorrel on General*
Longstreet after the Seven Days' Campaign

Boldness was prudence!

> —*General Longstreet on coming to the aid of*
> *Stonewall Jackson at Second Manassas*

I am sending you the guns, dear General. This is a hard fight, and we had better all die than lose it.

> —*General Longstreet to General Roger Pryor,*
> *Antietam*

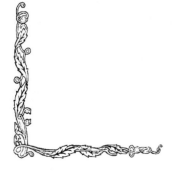
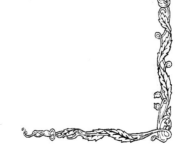

Longstreet's conduct on this great day of battle was magnificent. He seemed everywhere along his extended lines, and his tenacity and deep-set resolution, his inmost courage, which appeared to swell with the growing peril to the army, undoubtedly stimulated the troops to greater action, and held them in place despite all weakness.

—Brigadier General Moxley Sorrel on Longstreet under fire at Antietam

[Longstreet was] as cool and composed as
if on dress parade. I could discover no trace
of unusual excitement except that he
seemed to cut through his tobacco at each
chew.

*—J. W. Ratchford, aide to General D. H. Hill,
on General Longstreet at Antietam*

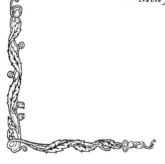

Look out for work now, boys, for here's the
old bulldog again.

*—Men from a Florida brigade on their way
to Gettysburg, as Longstreet passes*

By the soldiers he is invariably spoken of as the best fighter in the whole army.

—Lt. Col. Arthur Lyon Fremantle, Her Majesty's Coldstream Guards

Drive them, General. These western men can't stand it any better than the Yankees we left in Virginia. Drive 'em.

—General Longstreet to General Benjamin Humphreys at Chickamauga

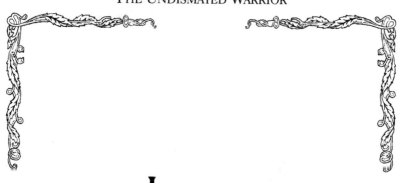

If we had our
Virginia army here,
we would have whipped
them in half the time.

—General Longstreet to Major William Owen
at Chattanooga

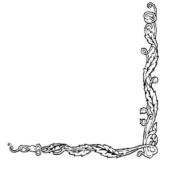

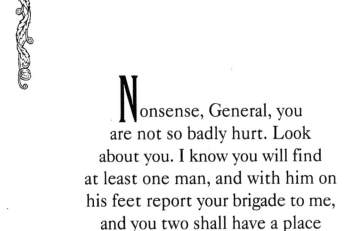

Nonsense, General, you
are not so badly hurt. Look
about you. I know you will find
at least one man, and with him on
his feet report your brigade to me,
and you two shall have a place
in the fighting-line.

*—General Longstreet to Brigadier
General Henry Benning at Chattanooga*

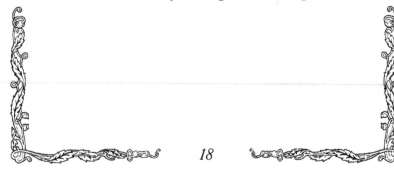

Longstreet is a bully general; he is a real bulldog fighter [and] he drives the Yankees whenever he meets them. He is a favorite of mine; I think he is next to General Lee. General Lee calls him his old war horse.

—A private serving under Stonewall Jackson
in February 1863

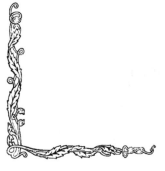

With the army, I shall be sure to be with it.

—General Longstreet to Harrison, the spy, when
asked where he could be found later

Joseph E. Johnston

CHAPTER THREE

The Art of War

General Longstreet wanted to save men's lives' not test their character. Risk had to be measured by cost. Careful and deliberate planning brought victory. But when the time came, Longstreet hit hard and fast.

Longstreet supported Lee's bold strategic moves, but he became increasingly committed to the tactical defensive. The defensive battles of Second Manassas and Fredericksburg were victorious struggles that saved men's lives. He could not

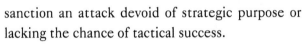

sanction an attack devoid of strategic purpose or lacking the chance of tactical success.

By 1863, Longstreet knew that Confederate troops numbered fewer than Federal forces and that his army's resources were limited. In the general's mind, strategy and tactics had to replace "muscle against muscle." He firmly believed their purpose should be to impair the morale of the Federal army and shake Northern confidence in its leaders.

Longstreet understood, perhaps better than any other commander, the art of war. He knew what was necessary to win and he knew how to use his assets to best advantage. More important, he knew how to count the cost; sometimes the price was just too high.

★ ★ ★

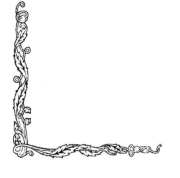

His forte though
as an officer consists, I
think, in the seeming ease
with which he can handle and
arrange large numbers of troops,
as also with the confidence and
enthusiasm with which he
seems to inspire
them.

*—Major Thomas Goree in a letter
to his mother, December 1861*

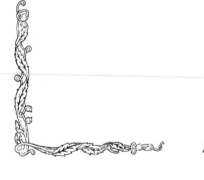

I suggested, as
the day was far spent,
that a reconnaissance in
force be made at nightfall to
the immediate front of the enemy,
and if an opening was found for an
entering wedge, that we have all
things in readiness at daylight
for a good day's work.

—*General Longstreet on Second Manassas*

Longstreet was seen at his best during the battle. His consummate ability in managing troops was well displayed that day and his large bodies of men were moved with great skill and without the least confusion.

—*Brigadier Moxley Sorrel on General Longstreet at Second Manassas*

If I had been in General Burnside's place, I would have asked the president to allow me to resign rather than execute his order to force the passage of the river and march the army against Lee in his stronghold.

—*General Longstreet on the Battle of Fredericksburg*

If we only save the finger of one man, that's enough.

—*General Longstreet at Fredericksburg*

The only hope we had was to outgeneral the Federals.

—*General Longstreet on the war in 1863*

If we could cross
the Potomac with one
hundred and fifty thousand men,
I think we could demand Lincoln to
declare his purpose. If it is a Christian
purpose, enough of blood has been shed
to satisfy any principles. If he intends
extermination, we should know it at
once and play a little at that game
whilst we can.

—*General Longstreet in a letter to*
Senator Louis Wigfall, May 1863

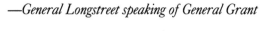

I would not give the life of a single soldier of mine for a barren victory.

—*General Longstreet to General Lee*

We must make up our minds to get into line of battle and to stay there; for that man will fight us every day and every hour till the end of this war. In order to whip him, we must outmaneuver him, and husband our strength as best we can.

—*General Longstreet speaking of General Grant*

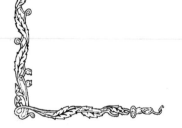

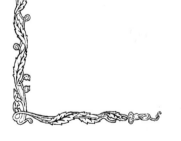

When the enemy was in sight, I was content to wait for the most favorable moment to strike—to estimate the chances, and even decline battle if I thought them against me.

—*General Longstreet in a newspaper interview*

We shall fight him [Grant] of course, as long as we have a man, but we should fight with much better heart, if we could hope of results.

—*General Longstreet to General Lee, February 1865*

General Beauregard

CHAPTER FOUR

Contemporaries in Gray

General Longstreet quickly won the recognition and favor of his superiors. General Johnston, General Beauregard, and General Lee all sought Longstreet as their second-in-command. Of the three commanders, General Lee was the one to see his wishes fulfilled.

Lee called Longstreet "the Staff of my right hand" and gave him much of the credit for their victories. By July 1862, Lee had determined that Longstreet should be his second-in-command and began to remove the four other officers who outranked him, leaving Longstreet the senior major general in Lee's army. General Lee divided his army into two corps. Longstreet was assigned five divisions and Stonewall Jackson was assigned three.

The soldiers who served under General Longstreet spoke of their commander with great affection and absolute confidence in his ability. Even those who later would be among his greatest accusers commended Longstreet for his superior military expertise. Jubal Early, Fitzhugh Lee, and John Gordon all talked of him with words of sincere praise.

Seen as brave, resolute and wise, Longstreet's reputation is a testament to the fact that the success of a great general is not only measured by victory on the hard-fought field, but by the respect and admiration of his comrades-in-arms.

I am satisfied he contributed very largely to the repulse of the enemy by his own personal exertions.

—General Jubal Early's official report after the battle at Blackburn Ford

I recollect well my thinking, there is a man that cannot be stampeded.

—General Fitzhugh Lee on General Longstreet at Bull Run

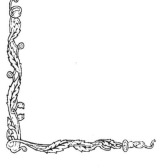

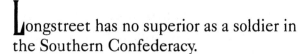

Longstreet has no superior as a soldier in the Southern Confederacy.

—*General Lafayette McLaws to General Richard Ewell*

I was a mere spectator, for General Longstreet's clear head and brave heart left me no apology for interference.

—*General Joseph Johnson in his report on Williamsburg*

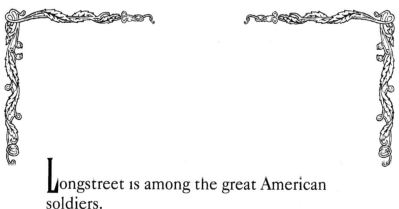

Longstreet is among the great American soldiers.

—*General John Gordon*

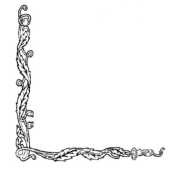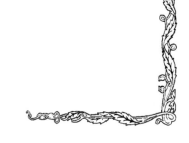

Next to Lee I should prefer entrusting the chief command of our armies to him.

—*William Petit, artilleryman, writing of Longstreet at Fredericksburg*

Longstreet is the man, boys, Longstreet is the man.

—*General John Breckinridge, the day after Chickamauga*

Longstreet then was the organizer of the victory on the Confederate side, and Thomas the savior of the army on the other side.

—*General D. H. Hill on General Longstreet*
at Chickamauga

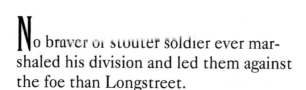

No braver or stouter soldier ever marshaled his division and led them against the foe than Longstreet.

—*Walter Taylor, Lee's staff officer*

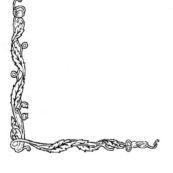

He was the first general I had met since my arrival who talked of victory.

—*General John Bell Hood on General Longstreet's*
arrival at Chickamauga

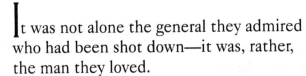

It was not alone the general they admired who had been shot down—it was, rather, the man they loved.

—Robert Stiles, an artillery officer, on the wounding of General Longstreet

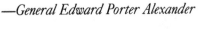

Longstreet's fall seemed actually to paralyze our whole corps.

—General Edward Porter Alexander

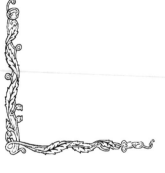

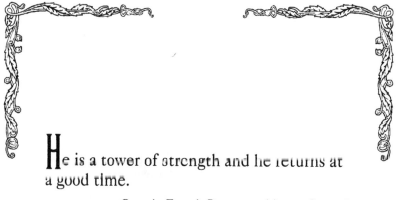

He is a tower of strength and he returns at a good time.

—*Captain Francis Dawson writing on General Longstreet's return to service*

Of all the men living, not excepting our incomparable Lee himself, I would rather follow James Longstreet in a forlorn help or desperate encounter against heavy odds. He was our hardest hitter.

—*General John Bell Hood*

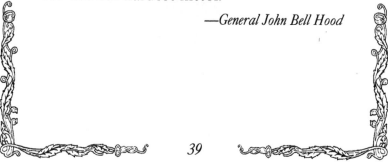

Stonewall Jackson

CHAPTER FIVE

Contemporaries in Blue

The men in blue who fought Longstreet on many a battlefield faced a general who proved to be a relentless and unyielding foe. Federal officers at Gettysburg and the Wilderness spoke of his bravery and tenacity. General Grant's and General Halleck's determination to drive him out of Tennessee testified to his prowess. President Lincoln also acknowledged Longstreet's military ability and effectiveness, even remarking that the general's death would bring an end to the war.

After the Confederate surrender, President

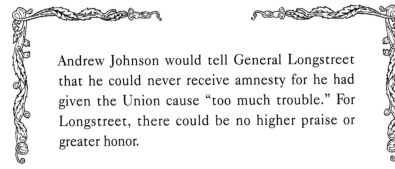

Andrew Johnson would tell General Longstreet
that he could never receive amnesty for he had
given the Union cause "too much trouble." For
Longstreet, there could be no higher praise or
greater honor.

★ ★ ★

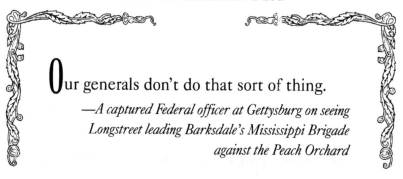

Our generals don't do that sort of thing.

> —*A captured Federal officer at Gettysburg on seeing*
> *Longstreet leading Barksdale's Mississippi Brigade*
> *against the Peach Orchard*

Longstreet's advice was sound military sense; it was the step I feared Lee would take.

> —*General George Meade on Longstreet's advice to*
> *General Lee at Gettysburg*

Julia Dent Grant: Now Ulysses, you know that you are not going to hurt Longstreet.

General U. S. Grant: I will if I can get him, he is bad company.

> —*December 1863*

Drive Longstreet out of Tennessee and keep him out.

—*General Henry Halleck to General John Foster,*
December 1863

If Longstreet is not driven out of the valley entirely, and the road destroyed east of Abingdon, I do not think it unlikely that the last great battle of the war will be fought in East Tennessee.

—*General Grant, December 1863*

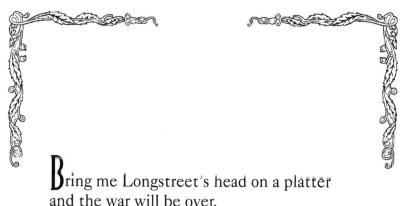

Bring me Longstreet's head on a platter and the war will be over.

—President Abraham Lincoln

It's no use to stop and fight Longstreet. You can't whip him. It don't make any difference, whether he has one man or a hundred thousand.

—General Gordon Granger, 1864

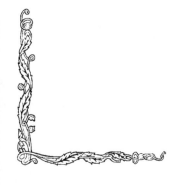

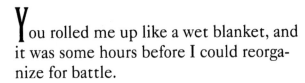

You rolled me up like a wet blanket, and it was some hours before I could reorganize for battle.

—*General Winfield Scott Hancock to General Longstreet
on the Battle at the Wilderness*

To kill Longstreet.

—*President Lincoln on the morning of the Battle of
the Wilderness when asked about the best thing that
could happen to the Union that day*

In the late rebellion, I think, not one charge was ever brought against General Longstreet for persecution of prisoners of war or of persons for their political opinions.

—*General Grant to President
Andrew Johnson*

There are three persons in the South who can never receive amnesty: Mr. Davis, General Lee and yourself. You have given the Union cause too much trouble.

—*President Andrew Johnson to General Longstreet regarding his pardon*

He was brave, honest, intelligent, a very capable soldier, subordinate to his superiors, just and kind to his subordinates, but jealous of his own rights which he had the courage to maintain.

—*General Grant*

General Robert E. Lee

CHAPTER SIX

Lee and Longstreet

General Lee and General Longstreet became
close friends and spent long hours together sharing
meals and conversation. Lee often sought advice
and counsel from his "old war horse" and principal
lieutenant.

Although Longstreet did not always agree with
his commander, there was never any question of
his loyalty and devotion. According to Colonel
Fremantel, you could not please Longstreet more
than by praising Lee.

Longstreet's friendship with Lee continued

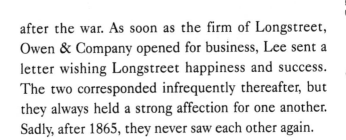

after the war. As soon as the firm of Longstreet, Owen & Company opened for business, Lee sent a letter wishing Longstreet happiness and success. The two corresponded infrequently thereafter, but they always held a strong affection for one another. Sadly, after 1865, they never saw each other again.

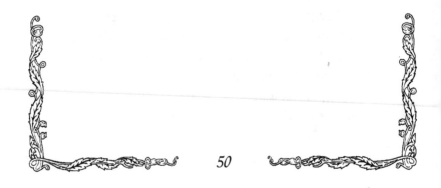

Longstreet is a capital soldier. His recommendations hitherto have been good, and I have confidence in him.

—General Lee shortly after assuming command

The staff of my right hand.

—General Lee of General Longstreet at the conclusion of the Seven Days' battles

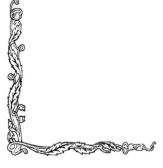

Ah here is Longstreet; here is my old war horse! Let us hear what he has to say.

—*General Lee as he embraces General Longstreet after the Battle of Antietam*

I only wish to do what I regard as my duty— give you the full benefit of my views.

—*General Longstreet to General Lee, April 1863*

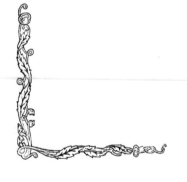

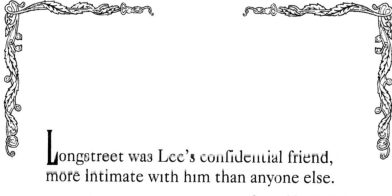

Longstreet was Lee's confidential friend, more intimate with him than anyone else.

—*General D. H. Hill*

Finish the work before you, my dear general, and return to me. I want you badly and you cannot get back too soon.

—*General Lee in a letter to General Longstreet five days after the battle of Chickamauga*

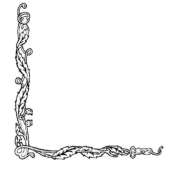
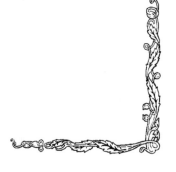

All that we have to be proud of has been accomplished under your eye and under your orders. Our affections for you are stronger, if it is possible for them to be stronger, than our admiration for you.

—General Longstreet in a letter to General Lee
from the western theater

I think he [Lee] relied very much on Longtreet, who was a great soldier, a very determined and fearless fighter.

—Raphael Moses, Longstreet's staff officer

Do not let Sherman capture you, and I will endeavor to hold Grant till you return.

—*General Lee in a letter to General Longstreet,*
August 1864

If you become as good a merchant as you were a soldier, I shall be content. No one will then excel you, and no one can wish you more success or more happiness than I. My interest and affection for you will never cease, and my prayers are always offered for your prosperity.

—*Lee writing to Longstreet after the war*

General Hill

CHAPTER SEVEN

Crossroads at Gettysburg

Little did General Longstreet know on July 1, 1863, that the Battle of Gettysburg would haunt him for the rest of his life. Longstreet issued protest after protest against an offensive attack on Cemetery Ridge. Even so, several years after Appomattox, the blame for the loss of Gettysburg, and consequently the entire war, would be laid at the general's feet.

Longstreet reached Seminary Ridge late in the afternoon of July 1, after the Confederate army had driven the Union troops off the field. The commander realized the Union army was in a good defensive position and suggested that the Confederates be content with the day's victory and seek a strong defensive position of their own. By so doing, Meade would be forced to do the attacking. To Longstreet's surprise, Lee announced his plan to attack the enemy where they stood the next day. General Lee believed an attack was unavoidable and would have a good chance for success.

The next morning, Longstreet proposed a flanking attack, but Lee would not be moved. When night fell, the Confederates had gained some ground, but the Union line was intact. Their odds would have been better had Longstreet's divisions not fought virtually alone. The assault was badly managed, with no concert of action between the three corps.

Lee viewed July 2 as a limited success and determined to renew the fight the next day. The following morning, he decided to assault Cemetery Ridge with Longstreet's corps preceded by a massive artillery barrage. Longstreet suggested that a frontal assault was unwise and could not succeed but Lee was unyielding. Longstreet made preparations for battle.

The attack lay in the hands of an officer who opposed it thoroughly. Longstreet carried out his orders with great reluctance but with his full talents and energy. He believed the attack would fail and that many lives would be lost. When the moment came for advance, he was unable to speak. He could only nod.

The advance began at approximately two o'clock, and by all accounts it was magnificent. In perfect order the gray ranks moved slowly across the valley, braving shell, grapeshot, and canister. They broke into a run only as they neared the crest of the ridge. But the assault was doomed, and the Confederates slowly returned under heavy fire.

Lee had failed, and more than 20,000 Southerners lay scattered across the Pennsylvania countryside as testimony to the high cost of war. To his troops Lee announced, "It is all my fault."

If he is there, it will be because he is anxious that we should attack him—a good reason, in my judgment, for not doing so.

—*General Longstreet to General Lee on his plan to attack Cemetery Ridge, July 1, 1863*

The general is a little nervous this morning; he wishes me to attack. I do not wish to do so without Pickett. I never like to go into battle with one boot off.

—*General Longstreet to General John Bell Hood, July 2, 1863*

His fine horsemanship as he rode, hat in hand, and martial figure, were most inspiring.

—*Brigadier Moxley Sorrel, on General Longstreet personally leading the attack on July 2, 1863*

The order for this attack, which I could not favor under better auspices, would have been revoked had I felt that I had that privilege.

—*General Longstreet's official report of the battle*

General, I have been a soldier all my life. I have been with soldiers, engaged in fights by couples, by squads, companies, regiments, divisions, and armies, and should know, as well as anyone, what soldiers can do. It is my opinion that no fifteen thousand men ever arrayed for battle can take that position.

—General Longstreet to General Lee, July 3, 1863

I do not want to make this charge. I do not see how it can succeed. I would not make it now but that General Lee has ordered it and is expecting it.

—General Longstreet to General E. P. Alexander,
July 3, 1863

During the firing
of the artillery Longstreet
rode slowly and alone immediately
in front of our entire line. He sat his
large charger with a magnificent grace
and composure I never before beheld.
His bearing was to me the grandest moral
spectacle of the war. I expected to see him
fall every instant. Still he moved on, slowly
and majestically with an inspiring confidence, composure, self-possession and
repressed power, in every movement
and look that fascinated me.

*—General James Kemper on General Longstreet
just prior to the charge, July 3, 1863*

I was convinced that he would be leading his troops to needless slaughter, and did not speak. I bowed my head in answer.

—General Longstreet on General Pickett's request to advance, July 3, 1863

Very well; never mind, then, General; just let them remain where they are. The enemy's going to advance, and will spare you the trouble.

—General Longstreet to General Pettigrew when he stated he was unable to bring his men up again after Pickett's charge, July 3, 1863

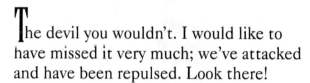

The devil you wouldn't. I would like to have missed it very much; we've attacked and have been repulsed. Look there!

> —*General Longstreet in reply to Lt. Col. Arthur Fremantle's statement that he wouldn't have missed the battle for anything, July 3, 1863*

That day at Gettysburg was one of the saddest of my life.

> —*General Longstreet on July 3, 1863*

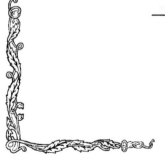

J. E. B. Stuart

CHAPTER EIGHT

The Unconquered

General Longstreet loosened his grip on his faithful sword only when General Lee had surrendered his shattered forces and there was no more fighting to be done.

On April 8, 1865, Brigadier General William Pendleton, the army's artillery commander, counseled Longstreet to urge Lee to surrender but Longstreet refused to speak of defeat.

Longstreet discussed the situation with his superior that night. Lee hoped to launch an attack the next morning. Longstreet, the undismayed

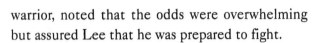

warrior, noted that the odds were overwhelming but assured Lee that he was prepared to fight.

The next day brought no hope for success, and Lee rode off to meet the Federal commander at Appomattox Court House. Longstreet's proud First Corps was the last of the Army of Northern Virginia to lay down its arms.

Lee and Longstreet parted company on April 12, 1865. Lee embraced Longstreet and asked Major Goree to look after him. With that, Lee took his leave and rode away on Traveller.

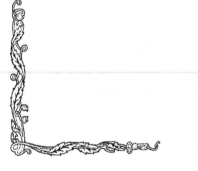

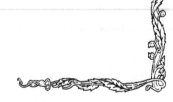

If General Lee doesn't know when to sur-render until I tell him, he will never know.

—*General Longstreet to General William Pendleton*
at Appomattox

You only have to give me the order, and the attack will be made in the morning.

—*General Longstreet to General Lee at Appomattox*

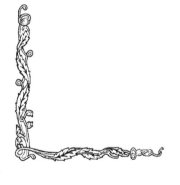

Not yet.

> —*General Longstreet to General Lee upon reading the*
> *note from Grant proposing surrender*

General, if he does not give us good
terms, come back and let us fight it out.

> —*General Longstreet's final counsel to General Lee*

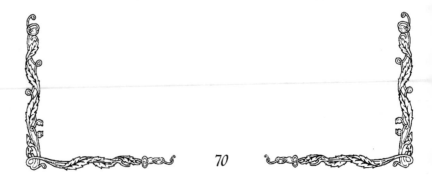

As you are now more reasonable, I will say that General Lee has gone to meet General Grant, and it is for them to determine the future of our armies.

—*General Longstreet to General George A. Custer at Appomattox in response to the demand that Longstreet surrender the Army of Northern Virginia, April 9, 1865*

Captain, I am going to put my old war horse under your charge. I want you to take good care of him.

—*General Lee to Major Thomas Goree on leaving General Longstreet at Appomattox*

General John Bell Hood

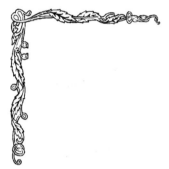

CHAPTER NINE

Lee's Tarnished Lieutenant

With the Confederate surrender at Appomattox, Longstreet henceforth saluted the Stars and Stripes unfailingly and devoted himself to the restoration of goodwill between the North and the South. He was brave enough to follow the path of duty as he saw it, no matter where it led.

During Reconstruction, Longstreet met the requirements of good citizenship in the restored Union in what he deemed the proper spirit and accepted an office at the hands of President Grant. His actions brought him political condemnation in the war-ravaged South. Of course, while General Lee still lived, Longstreet's detractors remained quiet, silenced by official records filled with letters of admiration and affection for Longstreet from Lee.

Longstreet's acceptance of a position under President Grant has always been misunderstood. Rather than a renunciation of his Southern sentiments or an act of disloyalty to the Southern people, he accepted Grant's offer in the belief that it was his duty to serve the public in an office that otherwise would be held by carpetbaggers and Rebel haters. But his decision was premature—the passions of the people were still too inflamed. Without understanding his motives, the Southerners he loved turned against him.

The most serious charge against Longstreet was that he had disobeyed orders at Gettysburg, causing defeat in the battle and the war. The official records never bore out any of these accusations. In fact, charges were not even brought until some years after the battle and General Lee's death. Thereafter, despite evidence to the contrary, general wisdom held that the Federal victory at Gettysburg was the result of Longstreet's disobedience.

He was slandered by his adversaries and branded a traitor for more than two decades. Nonetheless, Longstreet always believed that in time truth would set things straight and the real story of Gettysburg would clear his name.

★ ★ ★

No one has worked more than I, nor lost more. I think that the time has come for peace, and I am not willing to lose more blood or means in procuring it.

—*General Longstreet on his fear of a resurrection of the rebellion*

We are a conquered people with but one course left for wise men to pursue, and that is to accept the terms that are now offered by the conquerors. Let us accept the terms as we're in duty bound to do, and if there is a lack of good faith, let it be upon others.

—*From an article written by General Longstreet that appeared in the* New Orleans Times, *March 18, 1867*

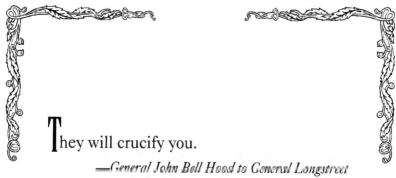

They will crucify you.

—*General John Bell Hood to General Longstreet*
upon hearing his plan to make a public avowal
of cooperation with the Republicans

I was anxious to keep the South out of the troubles that she has passed through since, and that was about the extent of my interest in affairs of state. For my pains, I had nothing of good from them, or even appreciative expression of sentiment.

—*General Longstreet in a letter to Thomas Goree*

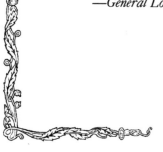

Grand old Longstreet! The rabble, the volatile, may hoot at and hound you for political errors which I deplore, but I will never cease to love, honor and admire you as one of the loftiest types of the truest heroism.

—*General James Kemper in a letter to E. Porter Alexander after the war*

Thirty years ago I was pilloried because I had so early cheerfully acquiesced in the result of the war, and accepted office at the hands of a Republican president, my personal friend and West Point school-mate, General Grant.

—*General Longstreet in an interview with Captain Leslie J. Perry*

My arm is paralyzed,
my voice that once could
be heard all along the lines is gone,
I can scarcely speak above a whisper;
my hearing is very much impaired, and
I sometimes feel as if I wish the end
would come; but I have some mis-
representations of my battles that
I wish to correct, so as to have
my record correct before
I die.

*—General Longstreet in a letter to
Raphael Moses*

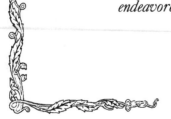

From this we know
that the ground of the Gettysburg
cemetery could have been occupied
without the loss of a man, yet even at
this late day, some of the Virginians, not
satisfied with the sacrifice already made,
wish that I, who would and could
have saved every man lost at
Gettysburg, should now
be shot to death.

*—General Longstreet on Meade's telegraph to
Halleck sent one hour before the attack on
July 2, 1863, in which Meade states he is
prepared to withdraw if the enemy
endeavored to move to his rear*

I do not fear the verdict of Gettysburg. Time sets all things right. Error lives but a day. Truth is eternal.

—*General Longstreet*

I loved and respected General Lee. I did not complain to him because of our Gettysburg failure. He never criticized my work there. His official reports and correspondence show that he fully approved my operations throughout. Our relations afterwards were as close as ever.

—*General Longstreet in an interview with Captain Leslie J. Perry*

Not one word appears to have been published openly accusing him of disobedience at Gettysburg until the man who could forever have silenced all criticism was in his grave—until the knightly soul of Robert Edward Lee had passed into eternity.

—*Helen Dortch Longstreet*

The soldiers of Longstreet's corps do not believe he disobeyed General Lee's orders at Gettysburg, or at any other time. We don't believe it now; we never did believe it; and we never will believe it.

—*W. H. Edwards, Washington, D.C.,* Star

Longstreet opposed Pickett's charge, and the failure shows he was right. All these damnable lies about Longstreet make me want to shoulder a musket and fight another war. They originated in politics by men not fit to untie his shoestrings. We soldiers on the firing line knew there was no greater fighter in the whole Confederate army than Longstreet. I am proud that I fought under him here. I know that Longstreet did not fail Lee at Gettysburg or anywhere else. I'll defend him as long as I live.

—*Captain O. Hooper, survivor of Pickett's charge, in an interview seventy-five years after the battle*

CHAPTER TEN

Farewell, Longstreet

On the morning of January 2, 1904, Longstreet became gravely ill with pneumonia. The end came swiftly and mercifully. He remained unconscious throughout most of the afternoon. About five o'-clock he stirred and whispered his last words.

The funeral was held on January 6. Once the service was concluded, pallbearers carried Longstreet's casket to a hearse and began the long procession to Alta Vista Cemetery in Gainesville, Georgia. State and local dignitaries, militia units, and Confederate veterans were among the many mourners who paid their last respects as church bells tolled. After the eulogy, a volley was fired over the grave and taps sounded through the cemetery.

Across the head and foot of the casket were placed a Confederate flag and a United States flag, the two flags the general loved so well.

As the pallbearers prepared to lower the casket, a Confederate veteran walked to the grave. He laid his old gray jacket and his enlistment papers on the lid of the coffin, and then stepped back. His comrades understood.

The grave closed over one of the greatest warriors the world has ever known.

★ ★ ★

I hope to live long enough to see my surviving comrades march side by side along Pennsylvania Avenue, and then I will die happy.

—*General Longstreet in a speech, Memorial Day, 1902, Washington, D.C.*

The Southern people have not appreciated you since the war, General, but when you are dead, they will build monuments to you.

—*An unknown Union officer to General Longstreet a few months before his death*

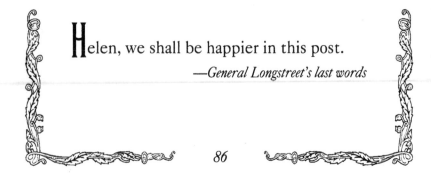

Helen, we shall be happier in this post.

—*General Longstreet's last words*

The hour does not clamor for the charity of silence, but for the white light of truth which I reverently undertake to throw upon the deeds of the commander who, from Manassas to Appomattox, was the strong right arm of the Confederate States Army.

I was writing for the love of him whose dear name and fame had been attacked; to place before his fading vision enduring appreciation of his valiant deeds as a soldier and high qualities as a gentleman. Providence decreed otherwise. While the opening chapters were running into type, the Great Captain on High called him hence, where he can at last have his wrongs on earth forever righted.

The warrior sleeps serenely today, undisturbed by all earthly contentions, the peace of God upon him. And I bring to his tomb this little leaf fragrant with my love, bedewed with my tears, heavy-weighted with my woe and desolation.

—*Preface to* Lee and Longstreet
at Gettysburg, *Helen Dortsch Longstreet,*
Gainesville, Georgia, August 1, 1904